9 Things You Must Know Before Starting a Business

Dennis Waller

Copyright © 2012 Dennis Waller

All rights reserved.

ISBN: 1479238899
ISBN-13: 978-1479238897

DEDICATION

To Bach Pham, thank you friend

CONTENTS

	Acknowledgments	i
1	You Must Have a Business Plan	1
2	You Must Have the Necessary Funding	5
3	You Must Have the Right People	9
4	You Must Have a Marketing & Internet Presence	11
5	You Must Charge What You're Worth	19
6	You Must Have Great Financial Management Skills	21
7	You Must Have the Right Business Structure	25
8	You Must be Able to Adapt to Change	27
9	Character Traits You Must Have to Succeed	31
10	About the Author	35

ACKNOWLEDGMENTS

"Time is the scarcest resource and unless it is managed nothing else can be managed."
-Peter Drucker

1 YOU MUST HAVE A BUSINESS PLAN

Before you do anything, you need to put together a plan. And I am not talking about just an idea or a concept but a full blown business plan. Developing a business plan is more than just a piece of paper; it is the heart and soul of the business. The process of developing your business plan requires a commitment to do the homework and the necessary research in order to know what you are going to do and how you are going to make it happen. In addition to the plan, you need to learn what your competition is doing. Be prepared to spend some time on gathering the needed information.

Consider your business plan like you would consider building a house. The first step would be to engage an Architect to draw a set of blueprints. No one in their right mind would start building a house without a clue as to what they are building. It is on the paper that potential problems show up. It is while the Architect is in the planning stages that issues are address and resolved. By the time the Architect is finished, all the trades will have a clear understanding of what is expected of them and know what materials are expected to be used in the process of building the house.

It is the same with a business plan. Just like the carpentry know what size the boards are going to be used on the building of the house, you too, need to know the basics of what it is that you are selling, whether it is a product or service, how you plan to money doing it and how to get the money you need to start. It is in the development of the plan that cost are determined and sell-points are created for the products. It is also during this time you get a grasp of the startup cost, capital needed, projections of overhead, cash flow and profit, and what sort of staff is required.

You have heard it said, "people judge a book by its cover." It is important to create an eye catching cover for your plan. Try to use imagery that conveys what your business is about. This will go a long way in holding the attention of a potential investor or a potential key member of your management team. Like a good book, have a great cover!

The Business plan should start with an Executive Summary outlining why you are qualified. Then a description of the company. Some of the basic ideas that need to be covered in the plan are the products and or services to be offered. The cost of the products and or services. The resources and cost for the product and how to bring the product to market. An understanding of the competition and knowing what price you can truly sell your product for. Developing a cost of overhead to determine your profit margin will help with setting prices.

There should be a financial statement and layout with projections of sales, profits, and cash flow. And there should be a section on the Marketing of not only the Product but the Company and You. Don't forget to include a section on Management if you are planning on having a team.

And lastly, there needs to be a "Mission Statement." Consider your mission statement to be the "why" you are in business in the first place. An example of the meaning of a simple statement could be something as " to provide a better product and or service at a better price than the competition in the marketplace."

Think about why you are starting a business to begin with. You know all the reasons, but there needs to be a statement that brings you into the role of not only servicing your community but strive to improve it too. Consider the greater good of the whole when drafting your mission statement. While we all want to make money, it is important not to compromise your values in the process.

When finished, the plan should be easy to read and understand. Try to use as many specific details as possible whenever you can. Work on it until you have it polished and looking professional. Now once you have it done, remember to create a "Confidential Agreement" for everyone to sign that you intend on giving a copy to. You do not want someone running off and using your hard work. Trust me, this happens all the time.

There is a story about a young man that wanted to open a restaurant on the town square in his town. Because of his age, so said the landlord, the landlord wanted to see the young man's business plan. The business was detailed down to a working menu with cost projections as to retail price and food cost. The young man failed to get a "Confidential Agreement" signed. Can you guess what happen next? The landlord told the young man that the space had been lease already and within a few weeks work started on the lease space. When the work was completed, not only did the landlord rip off the young man's plan, he even used the same menu and decor in the drawings the was included with the plan. Remember, have that agreement and be firm with everyone whom you give a copy of your plan to. It is up to you to protect your hard work.

So to recap. Your business plan should have a captivating cover that conveys your message. Your plan should include the following, an executive summary, a company description, the product or service offered, the management team, the market and competition, your marketing plan, financial statements, projected cash flows and projected profits, and lastly, your mission statement.

2 YOU MUST HAVE THE NECESSARY FUNDING

Lack of funding is one of the main reasons businesses fail. It doesn't matter if you are starting a business or expanding an existing one, Capital is King! With it, you have the ability to manage your business on your terms, without it, you are drowning. The first step is to get the capital needed to get your business going.

Now you have a business plan! If you are looking for outside investments or looking at going to a bank, this is where all that hard work pays off in putting in the time to create a killer business plan. The traditional forms of funding are Banks, Small Business Administration, and Venture Capitalist. Depending on your business model, there might be grants available, check into your local, state, and federal government for programs that offer grants for certain types of businesses.

When a potential investor looks at your financial statements and projections, they are interested in your forecast, cash requirements, cash flows, projected growth, balance sheets and most importantly, your ability to repay the loan. Remember to keep your expectations real and reasonable. Be able to back up the basis of your assumptions. Deal in logic and what is attainable in your market. You must show how you came up with the numbers you have. If you have done your homework, it will be easy to illustrate the assumptions and projections within your plan.

Either way, chances are your personal credit will be tied to your business. Be smart as any default on any business loans could be a disaster to your personal finances. Keep enough cash in reserve to cover short term debt. Choose the right options and take advantage of any money saving opportunities that might arise.

Don't give away the store in trying to attain funding. Nor give away the bottom line. First and foremost should be the economic health of the company. The terms of any agreement must fit the guidelines as set out in the plan. If your projections call for a payout within 3 to 5 years then stick to that. Never hope that sales will mysteriously jump through the roof just because you have a note coming due soon. Never agree to a interest rate that is detrimental to the business either. Learn what the market rates are for your type of loan.

Being new and not established in the business world can be difficult in trying to secure financing. The main stream avenues might not be for you such as banks and the Small Business Administration. Don't give up, consider other types of raising capital like including your personal savings, residential mortgages, home equity loans, or consumer loans. Don't be afraid to pitch your plan to family or friends. Another method is to borrow from private investors by contract. Think of borrowing from private investors by contract as issuing your own bonds. For instance, have a 5 year note at 10% simple interest with the interest payable quarterly with the principal due at the end of the contract. Get creative and remember to keep the interest rate reasonable.

Once you are up and running, keep some capital in reserve including the capacity to borrow. Be prepared for unforeseen events, emergencies, and opportunities because they will happen. The last thing you want to happen is to have a cash flow crunch. It will put a tremendous strain on sales and inventory because your need for immediate revenue becomes a daily crisis. At this point, there is no opportunity for sustained growth or well being. With a healthy cash flow you will make better decisions that are best for the company rather than just trying to keep your head above water. This principle is critical and you must master it, learn to manage your cash flow and debt.

In closing, in order to sell a investor on your plan, you need the confidence that you not only believe in your plan and yourself but you Know It! Act as if you know the results, act from the end. Have that level of confidence that sends a message that you are a sure bet. Investors can always relate to your passion and belief before they can relate to the numbers. Be that someone that everyone wants to be associated with, act the part of a winner. Perseverance is the key, don't give up! Investigate all sources of financing. If you have done the necessary homework and present it with style and confidence, the money will come.

3 YOU MUST HAVE THE RIGHT PEOPLE

You can have all the right pieces but if you don't have the right people to execute your plan, then you can expect to fail and fail miserably. Make sure you do your due diligence in hiring everyone from the kid that sweeps the floors to the general manager. Chemistry is important in putting together a team. Keep this in mind when hiring people.
This can be as challenging as securing financing. For every employee you hire, you are adding to the complexity of the staff. Remember to only hire employees that are essential to the business. Keep in mind that you are responsible for keeping a payroll at a manageable level. Keeping control on your labor cost helps with keeping a healthy cash flow.
I would recommend to stay away from hiring family at all cost. It is one thing to fire someone and never see them again versus firing someone only to go home and sit across from them at the dinner table. There have been wonderful families and marriages destroyed over working together in a work environment. Unless you have no choice, keep the family at home.
With employees come employee laws. Familiarize with the laws before hiring anyone. Keep in mind about the importance of a drug free work place. There are other considerations such as religious protection, racial discrimination, sexual harassment, child labor laws, civil rights, immigration, privacy, and Americans with disabilities. Do your research!

Depending on the size of your business, you might be exempt from some of these employee laws. Remember, the government is also concerned about who you don't hire. Create a hiring practice that is fair to you and your company while being fair and in compliance with the law.

When you do hire the right people, let them do their job. Don't interfere unless there is an issue that needs to address. Put yourself in their shoes and think about what you are going to say or do from their perspective. Is it something you would respond to in a positive manner? Think about what you are going to do before you do it. Think first, speak second.

If you get the right people, all you should have do to is be their coach. Remember, regardless of what you do, if you have employees, you are in the people business. If this is new to you, I would suggest on getting a few books on workplace psychology and reading them. With some thought you can put together an excellent winning team that will succeed.

4 YOU MUST HAVE A MARKETING AND INTERNET PRESENCE

You have the financing, you have the employees, you have a great product or service, now what? If people don't know about you or that you are open for business then you can't expect to have any business. This is where marketing comes in. A marketing plan is central to any business plan. Marketing helps you identify and target the customers you are after. This is one of the most important things you can do to ensure the profitability of your business. It is also one of the things that can bankrupt too if you don't have a plan that brings in results.

To get on the fast track look at what the leaders in your field are doing. Check out the marketing efforts of your competition. See what is working for them. Don't try to reinvent the wheel, rather model your plan after one that is proven. If they are an industry leader, there is a reason why. Learn what those reasons are and learn to model after their Success.

To begin with, you need a company name that tells the prospective customer what you offer. Your business name should tell your customer immediately who you are and what you do. Remember that your business name is your customer's first impression and you want to make a positive impression that last. Consider your company name to be the branding of your business. Put careful thought into the name you choose.

If you are selling plumbing supplies, then you should consider having that in the company name such as, "Metroplex Plumbing Supplies." This is common sense but it is amazing how many businesses pick a name because it is cute or catchy, but has no relevance to the business. If I asked you what does the company called, " Jeff's Lawnmower Repair." I bet you could guess what Jeff does. Now, how about a company called, "The Heritage House." Ah, now we have to guess, is it a museum? Is it a furniture store, or perhaps a art gallery? No, it is a candle shop. If the owner had named it, "Heritage House Candles," then there would be no confusion. Having a name that drives the point home and illustartes the purpose of your business is critical.

Another point to consider is joining the local Chamber of Commerce. Check with City Hall, chances are there are more than one Chamber you can join, especially if your town is in close proximity to other towns. Take advantage of the membership perks and attend all the meetings. Every meeting is an opportuntiy to gain exposure for you and your business. Network these meetings, like life, at times, it's who you know, not what you know.

Let's discuss the value of the internet. Almost any business can benefit from a web site. Having a web site spreads the word about your products or services. It makes it easy for potential customers to find you. It increases your visibility and works for you 24/7. A web site is one of the most cost effective ways to have a presence in the community. It can be used to announce your opening, market your products and services, create sales and sales leads.

The biggest benefit of a web site over the Yellow Pages is you do not have to wait till the next year for the new phone book to come out. And besides, phone books are becoming a thing of the past. More and more people are turning to the web for information. Managing a web site is becoming easier with the advancement of web tools like Wordpress and Yahoo Business. Now days, you don't need a PhD in computer science to build a professional looking site that is functional. And even if you don't have the skills, there are folks out there that can help you set up a site in no time. Craigslist is a great place to start for finding someone to assist you with building a web presence that you can be proud of.

Second, let's look at advertising. It will depend on your business model as to what strategies will work best for you. Whatever strategy you choose, whether it is direct marketing by mailing postcards or catalogs, door to door adverts, fliers, emails, promotional letters, or indirect marketing by participating in community events, engaging in public speaking or writing articles there are 3 basic price strategies to consider.

The first is called, "Market Penetration." Market penetration is done by launching a comprehensive advertising campaign, flooding the market by offering your product or service at a lower price than your competition. The downside to this strategy is it affects your bottom line by reducing your profit margin and worst, creating a customer base that will expect those lower prices after the advertising campaign ends. If you take this path it is important that you keep tabs on your competition to see how they react to your campaign. While this is an aggressive way to attract new customers and generate sales immediately, it can have adverse affects in the long run if not done properly.

If you decide to use this method I recommend that you use only one or two of your products or services as to not compromise the integrity of your entire product/service line when the sales promotion ends. It is fine to use a product as a "loss leader" to bring people through the door. A "loss leader" is where you sell a product at or near a loss to gain new customers to introduce them to your entire product line and your award winning customer service. Another way to consider a loss leader is like a "dollar menu" at a fast food restaurant. Half the battle is getting them through the door. Be careful to utilize this strategy with thoughtfulness and always be mindful to the bottom line.

The second strategy is called, "Skimming" This practice consist of taking the "high road." This isn't the best practice to use. While you have a really high profit margin on your products and services, it isn't a very effective method to attract new business for a new company. Unless you're the only kid on the block with the new toy, I recommend staying away from this strategy.

The third strategy is called, "Follow the Leader." This method is nothing more than following the market as it is set by the leaders in your field. This is a "reactionary method" of running a business. While we all need to be mindful of the marketplace, it is not good practice to let your competition set your price structure. In order to be successful with this method, you must keep control of your cost and maintain a healthy profit margin. If your competition gets wind of your practices and knows your margins, they can exploit you into bankruptcy.

The lesson is to learn a healthy balance between all three of these strategies. Know your market to know which products you can afford to go head to head with your competition and still make money and which products that you have a corner on so you set the market price and reap the benefits of having a proprietary product that is yours.

You see this game played every week with grocery stores with items that are advertised at a great price. While they all might be losing money on those bananas, rest assured that they are making it up somewhere else in the store. What you need to do is to review your product/service line to find what is unique to you and make that your selling point. Check out the competition to see what sets them apart from the rest. Find yours and make it your own!

Let me share with you a couple of stories where the business owner was able to identify a market and create a low cost method to tapping into it. There was a sports memorabilia shop in a suburb that had a hard time finding a way to get the word out that they were open for business. The owner discovered in his community that during the spring and fall the city supported little league baseball games at a city park that had 4 baseball diamonds. Leagues from surrounding towns played here because the faculties were better than any others and the city made a nice profit leasing out the fields. On any given Saturday, there would be over 40 games played. That is over 1,500 kids out there with their parents over the course of the day.

The Owner printed up a bunch or flyers and about every hour would go out to the park and distribute around a 100 or so flyers. At the end of the day, there would be about 1,000 of these flyers place into the hands of a captive audience. The flyers advertise that if you brought the flyer into the shop that Saturday, the holder of the flyer would receive a free baseball card of a star player from one of the local major league teams.

On average, about 100 people would come in and redeem the flyers. Out of those 100 people, about 80 would take the free card and leave. But, that left about

20 people that stayed and shopped at the store. The average sale for these 20 people was $30.00. Now I know that doesn't sound like much but look what happened. What is really interesting is on average, 5 of those people became regular customers that spent on average, a $100.00 a month.

So now some math. This weekly advertising campaign brought in 20 paying customers that added $600.00 in sales for the day. Out of that was 5 customers a week that spent on average a $100.00 a month. With just handing out these flyers, the owner was able to create and add $4,400.00 a month to his sales just off those 4 Saturdays. And the sales continued to compound as the season went on.

Now, for the cost of the campaign. The flyers ran him about 5 cents each to print and the free baseball cards cost another nickel if not free. On a average Saturday, his cost was about $55.00 or about $220.00 a month. Considering his profit margins compared to the "ROI," return on investment of the campaign, this was a highly successful advertising campaign. Granted, this is seasonal but he was able to convert 5 people a week for over two months in the spring and fall into regular customers for the entire year. And those customers brought in their friends and family too. On the labor, it wasn't really an additional cost as he already had a young man there on the payroll. He just simply sent him down to hand out the flyers that took hardly no time to do. While this is a unique situation, it shows how being creative with your marketing can add massive returns on your advertising budget.

Another story of a creative marketing plan that serves the owner and the community. This is about a man who opened up a Hair Salon in his town. Being new to the area and having tremendous competition he set out to make a name for himself. First, he went to the local Police and Fire Departments. As a token to their commitment to serve and protect, he offered free haircuts to all of them. His thought process was since he had no customer base, at least he would be busy cutting hair, thanking those who put their lives in harm's way to protect the community. Now the value of the haircuts was $20.00 and several of the police and firefighters took him up on the offer. Work quickly spread throughout city hall and in a joking manner, the Mayor asked where his free haircut was. The Hair stylist said, sure, no problem, matter of fact, how about a free haircut for the city council? The Mayor and a few of the members took him up on the offer and received a free haircut.

Can you imagine what happened? At the next city council meeting the Mayor made mention of his great looking haircut and the fact that someone in the community was showing their gratitude and appreciation for the service of the police and firefighters. Just that mentioning by the Mayor the council meeting made waves. It was on the local new, the city's web site and in the local paper. Thousands of dollars of free advertising from just that one event.

Now about the police and firefighters. Did you know that everyone of the men that got their hair cut was so moved by the act of kindness that they left tips that were far more generous than the average tip. In fact, some of the police and firefighters brought their families in for haircuts as well as telling their friends and extended family about the crazy barber who cut their hair for free.

With just this one simple strategy, the Hair Stylist was able to jump start his business and put him way ahead of the competition. He really didn't have any labor cost since in the beginning he had no business.

Since then, you better book an appointment two weeks in advance if you want to get your hair cut by him. And yes, he still gives haircuts to the police and firefighters for free and has made some great friends including the Mayor in the process. A great example of not only serving your own needs but those for the greater good of the community.

So to recap, find that something special about you, your products and services that you can make unique to you and market that angle. Get creative and think outside the box, in fact, throw the box away! Get out there today and make it your market, and Own It.

5 YOU MUST CHARGE WHAT YOU'RE WORTH

You must charge what you are worth for your services or products. The one thing I see more than anything else are business owners not charging enough for their products and services. This has to be the most common mistake made. One way this comes about is the inability to properly bid work, estimate cost or determining to correctly price your products and services due to a lack of understanding of cost. Yes, I understand that at times you need to have a "loss leader" to bring in new sales but even a "loss leader" should be kept under control with a clear understanding of the cost involved. It doesn't help to have great sales if you are losing money getting them.

It is imperative to have your pricing at a profitable level and still be competitive with your market. In order for your business to strive you need an understanding of fair market pricing in your area. Pricing your products and services incorrectly can be detrimental to your cash flow. Knowing how to price your products/services correctly and knowing when to offer discounts are keys to managing and growing your profits.

The positives of optimal pricing is raising your "ROI," return on investment, improving your short term cash flow and maximizing your profits. Be sure to check your price strategy often to ensure that you are current with the market and with your cost. When you re-evaluate check to see if the customer demand is still willing to pay for your products and services. Consider the effects of inflation or deflation if any on your price structure. Look at your competition to see if you are still competitive. Don't forget to use the internet to get an idea of prices throughout your market. And lastly, compare your wholesale cost to see if you are getting the best prices for your products and supplies. Saving a dollar is making a dollar so keep an eye on both sides of the sale to ensure maximum profits for you and your bottom line.

6 YOU MUST HAVE GREAT FINANCIAL MANAGEMENT SKILLS

If you want your business to succeed you must learn all you can about the basics of financial management. No matter how incredible you are at developing great products, developing great marketing strategies or running your business if you don't have a handle on the financials, the money will just slip away. Ignoring the financial aspects of your business is a guarantee that you will fail.

You must know how to effectively collect money and manage money. You must know how to manage your accounts, both accounts receivable and accounts payable. If you can at the very least, master the fundamental basics of financial management. If you do, your business will have a better chance of not only surviving but thriving.

By keeping a working knowledge of your daily sales and cost you'll be able to address issues before they become problems. Armed with this knowledge you'll be able to make better decisions about the day to day operations as well as long term goals for the company. If this is something that you just can't get your head around, or you feel you just don't have the time to deal with it, then go out and find someone who can. This is an area that you cannot afford to overlook or put off till later. There might not be any money later if you assume that everything will work itself out. Hire a CPA or a accountant. You will be surprise to discover how little it cost to have someone balance your books for you.

Think of money as the life blood of your business. Like life, if you have a serious cut or several small cuts, you can bleed to death. It is no different for a business. I know you have a respect and caring for your own personal health, have that same respect for the health of your company. Money is the life blood that your company depends on in order to strive and thrive.

Some of the basics that you need to familiarize yourself with are understanding basic bookkeeping, managing customer credit and collections, knowing how to analyze your financial state, and learning how to watch your expenses and cash flow.

Understanding basic bookkeeping is knowing how to manage your books or general ledger. This includes recording transactions, posting debits and credits, and preparing financial statements. It is also useful to know how to manage inventory, payroll, and keeping up with your bank statements.

Managing Customer Credit and Collections is managing your account receivables, this is critical to keeping a healthy cash flow. Also, it is important to know who you are giving credit to and keeping up with their accounts. Don't be afraid to ask customers to fill out a credit application. Remember what you went through to secure financing for your business? On the application ask for at least three trade references and at least one bank reference. Have a polite conversation about them and their business to get a better idea of who you are going to be giving credit to. Make sure to follow up with the information on the application to verify the information is correct. If you extend credit to them, ensure they fully understand your credit policy and terms. Create incentives to your customers for them to want to pay their invoices early. One way of doing this is offering 3/10Net30 on their purchases. This means they have 30 days to pay however if they pay within 10 days, they receive a 3% discount off their invoice.

On managing collections, be firm with your collection practices. Send out a reminder even if it is a short email or note and try to always keep it friendly. Don't expect your customers to always have you on their mind, instead send or email a statement when the payment is due. Remember, proper financial management skills along with successful collections can be the key to a successful business.

7 YOU MUST HAVE THE RIGHT BUSINESS STRUCTURE

One of the first decisions you will need to make in drafting your business plan is what type of business you are going to have and how to structure it. This is critical for tax purposes. This is where you will want to consult with an attorney or an accountant to discuss which business structure is best for your business model. The issues that will determine what structure is best for you will be based on the following, the simplicity of the operation, your exposure to lawsuits, the cost of registration, expected sales and profits, desired management level, the potential size and nature of business, and your exit strategy.

The typical structures for businesses are sole proprietorship, general partnership, joint venture, limited partnership, limited liability partnership; limited liability companies also known as a LLC, S corporation, C corporation, and Non Profits. Sole proprietorships, general partnerships, and joint ventures are considered to be the most simple to create from an operational standpoint. However with these types of structures, there are personal liabilities such as being responsible for the debts of the company.

If properly formed, corporations offer the shareholders protection from personal liability. S corporations are great for a "one man" business such as a consultant as there is only one level of tax on income. C corporations have two levels of taxes. One at the corporate level for income earned and another at the shareholder level for any dividends paid to them from the corporation.

If you decide to incorporate, it is important to consider which state to file in as there are different laws and requirements for the different states as well as registration fees. Select the state that is best suited for your needs. With as much work that goes into this aspect, it is smart to get some profession help. You want to ensure that you have the right business structure and it is done correctly. Look at your business structure as your body armour, you want the best, preferably something bullet proof.

8 YOU MUST BE ABLE TO ADAPT TO CHANGE

Why is this so important? Because if you cannot adapt to change you are certainly doom for failure at some point. We need to look at the past to understand this principle. Let's go back to the late 1970's when the first VCR's were introduced to the buying public. You seen an opportunity to get in on the ground floor of a business that was going to explode. And you were right; the demand for VCR's was incredible. You opened up a little shop to sell and service VCR's, because at nearly a thousand dollars each, people paid to have them repaired. And to supplement your business you added a TV repair too. From the start there was a debate about which format was better, Beta or VHS. So with additional capital you add another line of VCR's, the Beta line. It wasn't too many years later that it seem that the VHS was going to win out over the Beta, so slowly you started closing out your inventory of Beta VCR's. But there is another problem, the price is coming down on VCR's and people are not getting them repaired as before so your repair business starts to drop off. To make up the lost revenue you start carrying gaming consoles, TV's and Stereo's to complement your line of VCR's. Without really realizing it, you have transformed your little VCR sales and repair shop into an electronics store. Sales are improving and you are wanting to expand and grow so you start carrying Records and Cassette tapes to go with the stereo equipment. But there problems on the horizon, VCR's are on their way out and a new invention is taking over called

DVD's. Another problem rising along with these new DVD's is there is a new thing called CD's that are going to replace records and cassettes. So you start to close out your inventory of records, cassettes, VCR's and start putting money into the new DVD players and DVD's as well as these new CD's and CD players that are coming on the market. Your repair business is just about completely gone and you no longer take in new repair business, instead you sell them on new equipment because it is cheaper to replace than repair and the new electronics are being built better and lasting longer. About this time, with prices coming down and coverage becoming better you get into the newest fad, Cell Phones. You come up with additional capital and buy a franchise to be a dealer for one of the major cell phone providers. For some reason, stereo equipment sales are starting to die off and you start to close out your inventory. Now that the "big box stores" are carrying CD's and DVD's at a price point that makes them unprofitable for you to carry, you start to close them out. You realize that there is a ton of money in cell phones and they take up less space so you move to a better location that is smaller and offers a better opportunity to capture more of the cell phone market. You settle into this model and do rather well for years. Until one day someone ask you what it is that you do, and for a moment you remember that one time you were a VCR sales and repair shop but no longer. You don't even mention it because these kids today don't even know what you are talking about when you bring up VCR's. Wow, you take a step back and reflect on the last 30 years and see that you are nothing like you were when you started out all those years ago. All you did was go with the flow of the market and kept up with what the buying public wanted. You were able to adapt to the changes in the marketplace. Now imagine how long you have lasted if you did not adapt to change? Imagine where you would be if you stayed in the VCR business? Do you see how important it is to be able to adapt to change? It is important to be able to identify the changes in the market and change with it. Be an innovator and change with the times, that's how you secure new markets as they develop and you become a leader. Be aware of where your market is heading and stay ahead of it. You're not always going to pick the winners every time but with perseverance you will succeed. Don't be afraid of change! Learn to go with the flow, merrily as you go and you will succeed.

9 CHARACTER TRAITS YOU MUST HAVE TO SUCCEED

It takes a special person to become a successful entrepreneur. Maybe it is in being part gambler and part survivor, I don't know. However there is one common thread with successful entrepreneurs and that is their character. The most common trait is their ability to be a leader. A great leader is someone who can take control of a situation and turn it around while showing others the way. Great leaders are innovators because they must find a way that doesn't always exist within the framework at the time. A great leader is needed for the followers to be successful. It is a team effort that begins at the top. If the leader is unable to lead then as a group, they will fail.

Napoleon said that there were no bad soldiers, only bad generals.

Leaders are an interesting group of people to study. I encourage you to read books on great leaders and learn from them. To quote Napoleon on the importance of learning from great leaders he had this to say, "Read over and over again the campaigns of Alexander, Hannibal, Caesar. This is the only way to become a great general and master the secrets of the art of war." In a way business is war. You are at battle with your competition for a share of the market and you best know your terrain, your opponent, and your strengths and weaknesses.

Studying the great leaders in business such as Jack Welch, Andrew Carnegie, Henry Ford, and others, the one thing you will realize is they all have most of the following character traits. I have outlined a brief description of the most common traits among successful entrepreneurs here for your consideration. See how many you can match up to.

Passion- A strong enthusiasm and an intense desire to attain your goals. Someone who gets out of bed excited and ready to start the day. A person who truly believes in themselves and is enjoying life. This is the person who looks at their watch and goes, "Wow, it's 6:30 already, where did the day go?" Someone who is living their purpose in life.

Desire- To gladly make the greatest sacrifice to obtain a desired goal. An intense burning desire to get where they know they should be. This desire drives them to go above and beyond where most people would stop.

Decisiveness- The trait of resoluteness as evidenced by firmness of character or purpose. A person that can make up their mind and execute orders with confidence. Instils confidence in their employees by demonstrating a knowing of where they are going, of knowing the end game. Decisiveness is a true sign of leadership.

Determination- Reaching an unyielding position after careful consideration. Unwavering firmness of character or action. The word, "no" or "can't" isn't in their vocabulary. When things look hopeless, these people show strength in their resolve to overcome any obstacle. They are sure in their judgment.

Dedication- The act of binding yourself intellectually and emotionally to a goal. These are the people who will not be denied of their goals. Giving over exclusively to a single use or purpose.

Perseverance- To steadily persist in the direction of your goals withstanding discouragement or difficulty. The state or quality of being insistent when faced with obstacles or difficulties. To continue without halting.

Commitment- Loyalty to the attaining of your goals with faith and devotion. An act or course of action that is demanded of one. An engagement to assume an obligation. The state of being dedicated to a cause.

Compassion- Sympathetic. Concerned with human welfare and the alleviation of suffering. Humanitarian. The virtue of having empathy for others. The ability to show mercy. Having a sympathetic consciousness of others.

Patience- The capacity of enduring hardship or inconvenience without complaint. Realizing that we are all human. A state of endurance under difficult circumstances. Being steadfast. Patience is considered to be one of the most valuable virtues of life. The ability and willingness to suppress restlessness and annoyance when confronted with delays. Not to lose your temper.

Tolerance- Forbearing or lenient treatment. Charitable. An understanding of people. To be fair and objective when dealing with the opinions of others. Being respectful of others. The capacity to endure hardship.

Acceptance- The act or process of accepting. Ready and willing to receive new ideas. Having belief in something. Having the disposition to tolerate or accept people or situations. The ability to know what you can and cannot change and accept it.

ABOUT THE AUTHOR

Hi, I am Dennis Waller and congratulations for getting to the last page! You have shown several of the traits needed to become a successful entrepreneur such as the perseverance needed to read this book, the dedication required to see it through to the end, committed and determine to learn something new, and making the decision to buy this book in the first place. I hope that this endeavor has proven to be of some benefit to you in some way. If there were one piece of advice in parting it would be this, **"Live life independent of the good opinions of others. Listen to your inner voice and learn to follow your intuitive being."** Thank you for being a part of my world and don't let anyone tell you it can't be done!

Biography- Dennis Waller, author of several books, is recognized as an expert on spiritual experience, self-discovery, and exploring the human consciousness. As writer, speaker and philosopher, his teachings invoke an introspective view on how to discover one's true authentic self through a higher sense of consciousness and awareness. He teaches classes in the Dallas area on several subjects including Enochian Magic and Developing Your Psychic Abilities. He is best known for his work in the field of Indigos, people who possess unusual or supernatural abilities. His other fields of expertise include comparative religion, the law of attraction, and interpreting Eastern thought's relevancy to science and quantum physics. He is in demand as a guest speaker on radio programs, a lecturer at churches and life enrichment groups, and conducts workshops for Indigos.

www.ingramcontent.com/pod-product-compliance
Lightning Source LLC
Chambersburg PA
CBHW061520180526
45171CB00001B/267